SMOKIN'
RACE CARS

FAST WHEELS!

K. C. Kelley

Speeding Star
an imprint of
Enslow Publishers, Inc.

Library of Congress Cataloging-in-Publication Data

Kelley, K. C.
  Smokin' race cars / K.C. Kelley.
    pages cm. — (Fast wheels!)
  Previously titled: Hottest NASCAR machines
  Includes bibliographical references and index.
  Summary: "Experience the thrill of a NASCAR race, and learn about the cars, personalities, and races associated with this sport"—Provided by publisher.
  ISBN 978-1-62285-095-2
  1. NASCAR (Association)—History—Juvenile literature. 2. Stock car racing—United States—History—Juvenile literature. 3. Stock cars (Automobiles)—Juvenile literature. I. Title.
  GV1029.9.S74K4547 2013
  796.720973—dc23
                    2012048121

Future Editions
Paperback ISBN: 978-1-62285-096-9
EPUB ISBN: 978-1-62285-098-3
Single-User PDF ISBN: 978-1-62285-099-0
Multi-User PDF ISBN: 978-1-62285-162-1

Printed in the United States of America

072013 Lake Book Manufacturing, Inc., Melrose Park, IL

10 9 8 7 6 5 4 3 2 1

To Our Readers: We have done our best to make sure all Internet addresses in this book were active and appropriate when we went to press. However, the author and the Publisher have no control over, and assume no liability for, the material available on those Internet sites or on other Web sites they may link to. Any comments or suggestions can be sent by e-mail to comments@speedingstar.com or to the following address:

Speeding Star
Box 398, 40 Industrial Road
Berkeley Heights, NJ 07922
USA
www.speedingstar.com

CONTENTS

At the wave of the green flag, drivers know the race has begun. Hours after the start of the race, there is only one winner. At the 2012 Daytona 500, the victor was Matt Kenseth.

WHAT IS NASCAR?

Under a hot Florida sun at the Daytona International Speedway, the noise is incredible. You can hear the powerful roar of 43 mighty engines and hundreds of thousands of cheering fans. The speed is intense—cars fly around the 2.5-mile track at nearly 200 miles per hour! The 2012 Daytona 500, the most famous of the dozens of NASCAR races held each year, is nearing its end. Fans and drivers alike are waiting eagerly for the checkered flag to drop—and the winner to cross the finish line!

The colorful, powerful cars drive around the final turn, bumper to bumper, inches apart while moving at amazing speeds. Drivers battle for position, testing their nerves and skills to gain a split second or a few inches. The finish line is just ahead and it is down to three drivers out in front. The checkered flag waves overhead as the car passes by. At that moment, a huge roar erupts from the crowd and the race is over. The winner, driver Matt Kenseth in the No. 17 car, winds down during a victory lap. This Daytona 500 is over. The sights and sounds of the day are seared into the memories of the millions watching in person and on television.

BECOMING A TOP SPORT

From the early 1990s until the late 2000s, the National Association for Stock Car Auto Racing (NASCAR) shot upward in popularity. In some parts of the United States, it is still the No. 1 sport. The drivers have become national heroes, while the races draw enormous crowds and huge TV audiences at tracks from coast to coast.

It was not always like that. NASCAR began in the Deep South in the late 1930s and early 1940s. Fast-car fans began to gather at small, local dirt tracks. As those races grew in size, some of the track owners and drivers decided that getting organized would be a good idea.

In 1948 local driver William "Big Bill" France gathered all the top drivers in Daytona Beach, Florida. They created NASCAR, an organization to help their sport grow.

Today's drivers earn millions of dollars (the winner's prize at some top races can be more than $1 million). But none of the early NASCAR drivers earned their living just by racing. For some, their

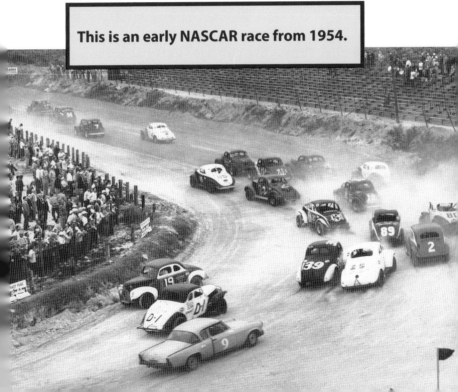

This is an early NASCAR race from 1954.

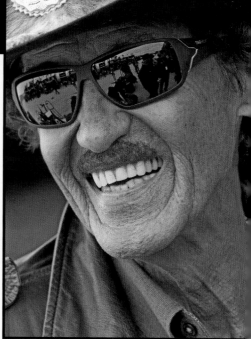

MEET THE KING!

Richard Petty is the most successful NASCAR driver of all time. He grew up around race cars. Petty's father, Lee, was one of the sport's early stars.

By the mid-1960s, the younger Petty was the best driver on the circuit. He won his first season title in 1964. In 1967, he won an astounding 27 races, still a single-year record. Around this time, Petty earned his nickname: "The King."

Petty won seven NASCAR championships, the most ever until the great Dale Earnhardt, Sr., tied that mark in 1994. When Petty retired in 1992, he had won an all-time record 200 races. Only one other racer, David Pearson, has won even half that many, with 105. Petty remained involved in NASCAR as a team owner for a while. His son Kyle was also a NASCAR driver.

race cars were the same ones they used to take the family to the store or to the movies. Drivers would sometimes just paint their car number on the side and head to the track. They drove "stock cars," which was another term for regular passenger cars.

Once at the track, the drivers were often their own mechanics, or brought along friends and family to help. They had to bring their own gas and gear, change their own tires, and fix anything that went wrong. Today's drivers have teams of dozens of people helping them out, on and off the track.

EARLY HEROES AND NEW TRACKS

Like today's drivers, the early driving heroes loved one thing more than anything else: driving fast. Lee Petty was an early hero, as were Curtis Turner and Herb Thomas. The Flock family of Alabama also featured several successful drivers. In one race, Tim, Fonty, and Bob Flock were joined at the starting line by their sister Ethel. They steered their big, heavy cars around dusty tracks at speeds

Early NASCAR driver Fonty Flock before a race in Daytona, Florida, in 1956.

NASCAR TODAY

The top level of NASCAR racing is currently called the Sprint Cup Series, after its major sponsor. Drivers in the Sprint Cup earn points for their finishing position in each race and for such things as leading laps in a race. After the first 26 races, drivers in the top twelve in points enter a special competition of ten races. These final ten races are known as the Chase for the Championship. In the ten races, those twelve drivers can earn additional points. After the final race, the driver with the most points is the NASCAR Sprint Cup champion.

Another division of NASCAR racing is the Nationwide Series. It is a proving ground for drivers who are preparing to step up to the Sprint Cup series.

NASCAR also organizes the Camping World Truck Series, where specially modified pickup trucks race on many of the same ovals as Sprint and Nationwide cars. Below these are several regional series held on smaller tracks. Drivers on these circuits hope to impress the team owners at higher levels.

above 100 miles per hour (mph). They were never afraid to bump into an opponent to gain an advantage in a tight race.

By the middle of the 1950s, NASCAR had grown. As more fans began to head to the racetracks to watch, more tracks were built. The first large paved oval track opened at Darlington, South Carolina, in 1950. In 1959, Bill France opened Daytona International Speedway. Before this superspeedway came along, cars raced at about 110 to 120 mph. But with the size of this track they could achieve speeds of 150 mph and above, which meant more exciting races.

NASCAR continued to grow bigger and bigger. Tracks were built in states such as California and New Hampshire—far away from NASCAR's roots in the South. Stars such as Richard Petty, David Pearson, Cale Yarborough, and Ned Jarrett became champions and heroes. In the 1980s, races began to be covered regularly by live TV. NASCAR reached an even wider audience. In the 1990s, NASCAR finally became one of America's top sports.

THE CARS OF NASCAR

Can just anyone head out to a local car dealership and pick up a NASCAR vehicle? The answer is no—but they can buy one that looks like the body of a NASCAR vehicle, such as a Chevrolet SS, Ford Fusion, or Toyota Tundra truck. The exterior designs of all the vehicles raced in NASCAR are based on models sold to everyday drivers. But that is where the similarity ends. All NASCAR vehicles are designed especially for racing.

From front to rear, a Sprint Cup car is packed with special features that turn these stock cars into super-fast racing cars.

ENGINE

The powerhouse that propels a Sprint Cup car is a 358-cubic-inch V-8. This engine is about 30

The stock cars of NASCAR are based on regular cars. This one, whipping around the track with Tony Stewart at the wheel, is based on a Chevy Impala.

to 40 percent larger than the engine in a typical passenger car. "V-8" means that it has eight pistons, arranged in a V-shape. These move up and down rapidly to turn the driveshaft, which helps to turn the wheels.

This engine can produce 865 horsepower (hp). Horsepower is a measure of engine performance, comparing the power created by one horse to what the engine can do. This means it would take 865 horses working together to produce enough power to drive a Nextel Cup car at top speed!

CHASSIS

Designed with the help of computers, wind tunnels, and endless testing, the chassis (CHASS-ee) is like the skeleton of the car. It is made of thick steel tubes welded together. It is designed to be strong enough to protect the driver as well as to support the heavy engine.

The chassis, or skeleton, of a NASCAR truck is shown here without the body.

BODY

The shape of a Sprint Cup car is carefully controlled by NASCAR officials. All teams must use the same body types, and for each body type, the cars must be built exactly the same. Officials use special measuring devices to make sure all teams are using the same shape of a certain car. Why all the rules? Because a car's shape affects how it moves through the air. That can greatly affect how fast it goes. Making sure that all the cars move the same way puts the emphasis on engine performance and driver skill.

COCKPIT

The driver's compartment is called the cockpit. There is room for only one person in this car—there are no back seats. On the dashboard in front of the driver are switches and gauges. They help the driver control parts of the car, and also let him see such things as how hot the engine is and how much power is in the battery. The steering wheel is much smaller than in a regular passenger car. It is easily removable, too. This allows the driver to

NASCAR officials measure every part of a car before giving it the "OK" to race.

climb into and out of the seat, which is very close to the steering wheel.

Next to the steering wheel is the gear shift lever. Having different gears helps car engines move more safely to higher speeds. Without gears, car engines would overheat very quickly by powering up too fast.

Finally, a radio button is located on the steering wheel. The radio, which includes earphones and a helmet microphone, allows the driver to communicate with his pit crew.

ACCESSORIES

There are not many! Sprint Cup cars have no doors—drivers climb in through window openings. There are no side windows, only netting. There is no speedometer, either—the driver must figure out the car's speed by reading the engine revolutions per minute (rpm's). And, of course, there is no stereo system. It would be too loud in the car to hear music, anyway!

A DAY AT THE RACES

A NASCAR race day is colorful, noisy, crowded—and for real fans, a little slice of heaven. At tracks around the country, a typical Sunday race draws more than 100,000 fans. Larger tracks such as Daytona or Talladega (in Alabama) regularly see crowds of more than 200,000 people. They fill the stands that surround the track and also cover the infield (the central area inside the track).

Race weekend starts Thursday or Friday for most NASCAR teams. Crews spend the day unloading cars, engines, tools, spare parts, and other gear. Drivers usually run practice laps in their race cars in front of empty stands that will soon be filled with cheering fans.

Crews unload their race cars and all the parts and supplies they will need before the race starts.

Qualifying is often held on Friday afternoon or Saturday morning. To determine the starting order of the race, each driver runs a certain number of qualifying laps, depending on the track. The drivers with the highest speeds will get the best starting positions for the race, near the front of the field. NASCAR races start with 21 rows of two cars each, with one car in a final row. This forms a 43-car starting "grid."

Crews then go over their cars inch by inch, making tiny adjustments based on computer tests and driver input. They might tighten the steering or adjust the balance of the wheels. It is all in an effort to coax every last bit of speed out their car.

THE RACES BEGIN

Friday and Saturday are when many fans start to arrive. Hundreds drive their motor homes onto the infield, where they will spend the weekend barbecuing, seeing friends, and watching the race up close.

Saturday of race weekend often means a Nationwide Series race at the track. For many

THE PIT CREW

Drivers make several pit stops during every race to get new tires put on their cars and to get refueled. Each of the seven pit crew members has a particular job. The best crews can change four tires and fill the gas tank in about 13 to 15 seconds!

Catch-can man:

This crew member uses a catch-can to catch any excess fuel that overflows from the car. He or she also takes the first emptied gas can from the gas man so a second can of fuel can be put into the car.

Gas man: Wearing special fire-resistant clothes, the gas man pours gas into the valve at the rear of the car.

Tire carriers: These two crew members carry the 80-pound tires to their new places and hang them after they remove the old tires.

Tire changers: With air-powered wrenches, these two members of the pit crew remove the five lug nuts that hold each tire in place. They then put five new nuts on the new tire after it is hung by the tire carriers.

Jack man: Using a large car jack, the jack man lifts the car so the tires can be changed.

Nationwide drivers, this is the highlight of their weekend. If they do well in these races, they may catch the eye of team owners looking for drivers to move up to the Sprint Cup series.

With the Sprint cars fine-tuned and the drivers rested and ready, Sunday dawns—race day. Drivers attend a morning safety meeting with track officials to go over the day's routine and rules. Crews are busy readying the car for the starting grid. To save gas and to prevent extra wear and tear on engines, the cars are pushed, not driven, into their places on the starting grid on pit road.

At many tracks, the drivers are introduced one by one on a stage. A stage set up at the start-finish line might be as much as a mile away from fans on the other side of the track. So large video screens help them keep up with the action and ceremonies.

After driver introductions, drivers stand by their cars while crews line pit road. Their uniforms form a rainbow of colors 43 teams strong. The national anthem and other music is performed. At some races, military jets roar by overhead, their engines challenging the sound about to erupt from the race cars.

START YOUR ENGINES!

Soon the drivers hear the most famous words in car racing: "Start your engines!" The drivers push a button that sends their mighty engines roaring to life. Forty-three 850-hp blocks of iron blast their sound into the air. The race is just minutes away.

The pace car roars out onto the track, and the cars in the starting grid leave pit road and follow slowly along. NASCAR races use a rolling start. That is, the race begins while the cars are already moving. The pace car "sets the pace," letting all the cars get up to the same speed. The pace car leads the field for a number of laps, and then quickly peels into pit road to get out of the way. As the cars reach the starting line on the third pace lap, the green flag drops and, in a heartbeat, the cars are almost flying down the track, heading into the first turn.

If you have ever been near a jet engine when it takes off, you know the feeling of having your

WATCH THOSE FLAGS

Officials at the start-finish line wave flags to indicate events during a race. Different flags mean different things:

 START racing! Or start again after a stoppage or slowdown.

 Take CAUTION. Everyone must slow down to the same speed after a crash to let debris (broken car parts) be cleared from the track.

 STOP! All cars must stop, and go to an area determined by a NASCAR official. The race might be stopped for sudden bad weather or other emergencies.

 Busted! A rule has been broken. The driver or team that broke the rule must go to its pit stall to wait out a PENALTY of one or more laps.

 Slower drivers who are a lap or more behind are about to be passed by faster cars. They must MOVE OUT OF THE WAY and let the faster cars pass safely.

 It is the LAST LAP of the race.

 The END OF THE RACE! This is the flag every driver wants to see first. It is waved when the winner crosses the finish line.

The black and gold pace car gets the cars up to speed before a race at Bristol Motor Speedway in 2011.

insides wiggle and vibrate with the force of the sound. That is what it is like at the start of a NASCAR race—and it goes on like that for hours!

During the race, fans can keep track of the action, as well as their favorite drivers, by buying special headphones on which they can hear track announcers. They also view video screens and look

RACE DAY SUPPLIES

Each NASCAR team has an 18-wheeler, called a hauler, loaded with gear that they move from track to track. For a weekend of racing, a team has an amazing amount of gear in their trailer:

- two or three race cars

- spare car body parts

- an extra engine

- virtually every engine part

- hundreds of tools of all sorts

- clothing for all the crew members

Goodyear provides tires to each team. Most teams also have several motor homes that are used by the driver and crew members at the track, as a place to rest and eat meals. It is like moving an entire garage and a car dealership in a weekend!

at the scoring towers, to see the always-changing order of the cars in the race.

The action speeds up and slows down, depending on caution laps (when an accident stops or slows the action on the track) and pit stops (when cars stop in pit stalls to get new tires and more gas). But most of the time it is all-out racing. Few events in sports are as emotionally powerful and physically draining as a NASCAR race. If you ever get the chance to go, grab it—and bring your earplugs!

OFFICIALS IN WHITE

On the side of the track and in the pits, TV viewers might see people in white jumpsuits, often wearing racing helmets. These are not drivers looking for their rides— they are NASCAR officials. Dozens of officials work each race, supervising pit crews, mechanics, and drivers to make sure that all rules are followed. They have the power to hold a car in the pits for doing something wrong or to report violations to top race officials for later penalties.

ON THE TRACK

Driving a NASCAR vehicle is easy, right? You just climb in, strap on your helmet, put the pedal to the metal and turn left for three hours. Not exactly! It is more complicated than that. There is much more going on inside the cockpit . . . and under the helmet.

The driver is strapped tightly into the seat, hands gripping the steering wheel. As the green flag drops, the driver stomps on the gas pedal, quickly shifting through the gears to reach top speed. The noise is incredible, but the driver's ears are protected by a thick helmet and earplugs. The vibration, however, is something the driver just has to get used to. At the speeds these cars are moving, every little bump on the track, or from another car, rattles through the nearly pad-less car.

Drivers have to cope with temperatures as high as 120 degrees. Their boots are lined with heat-resistant material, since the heat from the engine can sometimes melt the rubber soles. They get no meal breaks, no bathroom breaks, and no time outs. They might get something to drink during a pit stop, but that is all.

Some people argue that race car drivers are not real athletes. Those people have never spent

Strapped into his car with all of his gear on, Greg Biffle is ready for the race to begin.

be able to hold the car in a tight turn at high speed. They can also use a technique called "drafting." Drafting is following very closely behind another car. By keeping their car just inches behind another car, drivers can give their engines a bit of a break. The car in front is "cutting through" the air, making the second car's ride smoother. Drivers make dozens of these decisions every moment during a race.

They also watch up ahead. A puff of smoke half a mile up the track might mean an accident, so drivers must be ready to avoid trouble quickly. They want to do this without reducing their speed, if possible. They are also on the radio with their crews, figuring out when they should come in for a pit stop.

IN THE PIT

When it is time for a pit stop, a driver enters pit road from the main track. The car slows almost instantly from more than 150 mph to as little as 30 mph, depending on the track. The driver parks the car, engine running, in its pit stall. Then, like

TYPES OF TRACKS

Bristol Motor Speedway

NASCAR races are held on several types of tracks. The tracks are of different lengths, and the races held on them range from 350 to 600 miles. The name of a race often tells the length of the race, such as the Daytona 500 (500 miles).

Superspeedway: An oval track of 2.0 miles or longer. For NASCAR races, there are six of these tracks, including Talladega Superspeedway.

Intermediate: An oval track of 1.0 to 2.0 miles. Most NASCAR tracks are in this category. There are currently eleven of these tracks registered to NASCAR.

Short track: An oval track of less than one mile. Bristol in Tennessee is an example. There are six of these tracks.

Road course: A longer, twisting, narrower track consisting of right- and left-hand turns instead of only left-handed turns. There are dozens of road courses, but only four that are registered for NASCAR races. Sonoma Raceway in California is one of them.

Sonoma Raceway

Talledega Superspeedway

WHAT'S WITH ALL THE DECALS?

Your family car might have a couple of bumper stickers, but NASCAR vehicles do not stop there. They are almost completely covered by colorful decals. Why? One word: money! Every one of the decals on a NASCAR vehicle means money for the team owner. Teams sell sponsorships and use that money to buy equipment and pay employees. In turn, the sponsor's company is advertised on the car.

The more money a sponsor pays, the bigger the decal. Some sponsors buy space on all the cars, while others put all their money muscle behind one driver. You might hear a driver say that his "DuPont Hendrick Motorsports Chevy ran really well today." Every time the sponsor's name is mentioned, it makes it easier for a team to sell more sponsorships. Drivers get most of the attention, but sponsors are a key part of any NASCAR team.

having a lot more victories before his career is over! Stewart's background in Indy cars, another form of racing, helped him become one of the only drivers to race in the Indy 500 and a NASCAR race on the same day!

Jimmie Johnson: Most NASCAR racers are from the South, but Johnson grew up in California. He got his start racing motorcycles and dune buggies in desert races. He won his first NASCAR championship in 2006 after finishing second in 2005. In fact, he won five consecutive championships from 2006 through 2010. His five career titles are 3rd all-time, trailing only Richard Petty and Dale Earnhardt. They each have seven championships.

Matt Kenseth: Kenseth grew up in Wisconsin and started racing on small tracks there. In 2003, he became a part of NASCAR history when he won his first NASCAR title. Since then, he has finished in the top 10 seven out of the nine years until the end of 2012.

Dale Earnhardt, Jr., is one of the most popular drivers in NASCAR.

Dale Earnhardt, Jr.: The son of Dale Earnhardt, Sr., was voted by fans as NASCAR's most popular driver ten years in a row. Dale, Jr., in his old red No. 8 car and his newer No. 88 car, has had some success on the track. But not as much as his devoted fans would like. He has won 19 career races going into 2013 and even won the 2004 Daytona 500. Still, he's yet to have finished higher than third in a season.

Brad Keselowski: Keselowski has been racing for NASCAR since he was twenty years old. He started in the Camping World Truck Series and then raced in the Nationwide series. In 2010, he captured his first Nationwide title. He began to make an impact in 2011 when he finished fifth in the Spring Cup points standings. In 2012, he won five races and the series championship!

DALE EARNHARDT, SR.

The man who is perhaps the most famous driver in NASCAR history has not been in a race since February 18, 2001. That day, seven-time series champion Dale Earnhardt, Sr., was killed during a crash on the last lap of the Daytona 500.
Earnhardt's death stunned the NASCAR community. He was beloved by nearly all its fans, both for his success on the track and the hard-charging, bumper-bumping way he had won his titles.

Such accidents are sometimes a part of NASCAR. Drivers accept the risk while working hard to avoid trouble. Even more safety measures have been added as a result of Earnhardt's crash, from the HANS device to padded walls at some tracks.

Any souvenir featuring the black No. 3 car Dale, Sr., drove remains among the most popular in NASCAR. The legend of "The Man in Black" will never die.

INDEX